All We Are Told Not to Touch

New Women's Voices Series, No. 169

poems by

Leticia Del Toro

Finishing Line Press
Georgetown, Kentucky

All We Are Told Not to Touch

poems by Leticia Del Toro

Copyright © 2023 by Leticia Del Toro
ISBN 979-8-88838-026-0 First Edition
All rights reserved under International and Pan-American Copyright Conventions. No part of this book may be reproduced in any manner whatsoever without written permission from the publisher, except in the case of brief quotations embodied in critical articles and reviews.

ACKNOWLEDGMENTS

Many thanks to the editors of these publications, where some poems appeared in earlier forms:

Cipactli: "In Bermeo at Dusk," "Cara a Cara," "The Wailing"
Drum Voices Review: "Cuatro Caminos"
Konch Magazine: "Bougainvilleas"
La Raiz Magazine: "Just Outside the Gate"
Louis Liard: "Burning Cane"
rkVry Magazine: "Alive at Lampedusa"

Publisher: Leah Huete de Maines
Editor: Christen Kincaid
Cover Art: MAESTRAPEACE Mural, Detail of Yemayá ©1994 and 2000, Juana Alicia, Miranda Bergman, Edythe Boone, Susan Kelk Cervantes, Meera Desai, Yvonne Littleton, and Irene Perez, All Rights Reserved
Author Photo: Jacqueline Neuwirth
Cover Design: Elizabeth Maines McCleavy

Order online: www.finishinglinepress.com
    also available on amazon.com

Author inquiries and mail orders:
Finishing Line Press
PO Box 1626
Georgetown, Kentucky 40324
USA

Table of Contents

Cuatro Caminos 1

What Would Diego Paint? 2

Alive at Lampedusa 4

Bougainvilleas 6

The Wailing 11

Cara a Cara 13

Playa Cuastecomate 16

Burning Cane 17

In Bermeo at Dusk 19

Ser Madre 21

To Be a Mother 23

Just Outside the Gate 25

Shine 27

Relumbre 28

January Jicama 29

*These poems are dedicated to
Josefina Del Toro
María Guadalupe Díaz
Acela Preciado
Refugio Montes de Oca
and all the mothers before them*

Cuatro Caminos

Here is the photo, December 1974
Abuela stoic in the center
with a beach palapa background.
We are grouped around her, eight of us
in striped swim trunks, paisley bikinis.
I wear a navy blue skirted one-piece
and carry a blonde Baby Alive.

My mother hangs her arms around Abuela
bright in an orange tank dress, la quiere chiquear.
Abuela is draped in her rebozo at the beach,
replanted like a tree for our December holiday.

Later I will play with her braids,
she will let me unplait the crown she wears.
I will marvel at the length and blackness,
the old face that is my mother's,
the laughter and the Indian words,
like "*zúmbale*" when she sends me
running when it's time for the bathroom.

She will not enter the waves, fears the coastline
will plead for return to rustic rooms
guarded with songbirds near the cane fields.
My father will stay at her house two hours
as a gesture, but I eat everything she gives me.
Squash from a tin cup with chile
tortillas with fresh requesón
corn roasted to a char on a thin comal.
La quiero chiquear, I ask to bring her home.

We will live with this photo yearlong
until we make the trek to see her again.
Brothers and sisters, learn to drive, take diplomas,
discover the Isleys and EWF.
They will not dance to cumbias or eat tripitas.
The station wagon does not refill, for
the miles between Crockett and Zapotiltic.
I will return to the cane fields, to memorize her face,
the smell of the land, the sleight of the unmarked roads.

What Would Diego Paint?
    for the 43 from Ayotzinapa / para los 43 de Ayotzinapa

Five days ago I watched via computer screen
the green A marked on the palace doors,
sprayed, then ignited
bright fierce anger of youth ablaze.
Unthinkable, this the center of my family's country
but then the grandeur of the Palacio gave me pause

Who in Mexico could truly claim it?
Who did it protect? Who sought refuge there?
I once saw myself on the Palacio's walls,
in the faces of the indios that Diego painted.
What would Diego paint now? For who
will claim the bloody mural that is Iguala?
Might it matter as I live in this Estados Unidos....
removed?

A country that turns its back to the border
and whispers, dig, dig with your sun-seared hands,
move the earth and get here, ride the Beast,
take your chance, venture the river.
I cling to the roof over my head, alright
I am one generation away from campesina.
I only know hunger, second-hand
the hand that overfed me, Hostess cupcakes
and Gansitos, but mostly ranitas and taquitos
de chorizo, anything you want mija, any antojito
don't go hungry, mija, don't go hungry.

The only hunger that hollows me now
is the need to see my primos again
to sweep my grandmother's grave
and share some nopalitos in her home
to hold my primos' hands and faces,
and see our mirrored bones.

In my mother's earliest memory,
she huddles with her sister beneath a tree
un gran encinal at nightfall.
My mamá lived beneath a tree

the wind through dancing leaves, a lullabye
small patches of luz de luna
I think of that great oak, wish I could find it
to say thank you for sheltering my mother.

How many paisas still credit the hills,
los valles, una barranca as their
touchstones to home?
When all you have is the speed with which you flee,
you pray for some small shelter, a plate to scrape dry,
fight the roaring in your ears to roam,
so you venture, un esfuerzo
for my family you say.

They are burning the doors of el Palacio
because they have never had their own,
a defense, a partition, a patrimonio,
un domicilio, that sweet
safe place unknown.

Alive at Lampedusa

On radio breaking news of drowning at Lampedusa
It is not a name I know, but sound bites of *Italian coast
Roman mayor, deadly seas*, bring to mind so many
refugee ships ... I'm thinking of Elián
I'm thinking of Cuba, of Ceuta and death by water
or death by desert, which is more inhumane?
Why does this report break my heart today?
Is it the exotic port name? Or the thought of Eritrean
souls downed in the Mediterranean?
I once saw Euro tourists ferried with their cars
to islands of sumptuous beauty
Corsica, Sardinia, Sicily, playgrounds for europeos
now haunted by Yemaya's children.

I am the daughter of a man who at age fourteen
walked the desert for days, sun-sick and weakened
He took blows to the head then woke up in jail
to the broomstick beating of an elderly man.
When my father died at seventy-seven,
now alone in his own kind of frailty
his house was empty except for a Bible,
a typewriter, and notes of his own crossing at Yuma.

I have been one to covet summer sands among
the crowded Côte d'Azur, what is that luxury worth?
Will we not see their faces in the waves?
Where does nationality go when the body disappears?
They are fellow citizens of my
paisas in the desert, the unnamed but numbered,
How is it that we house the dead in modern stateside morgues
but we cannot shelter the living, we cannot offer a hand?
When a child suckling her mother's milk empties
the right breast, does she not move on to the left?
Are we not free to search our Madre Tierra
as free to search and settle, in her fertile curves?

Refugees who survived the fire on the waters
did not stay put in their shelters, in spite of
welcome kits of deodorant and toothpaste.

Officials were astounded by those who fled
to run free is to know you're hunted
but what is worse? Death by drowning on a fiery ship
or death by heat and fortified funneling through hell
of bracken fields and barren waste that ends in Pima county?

To be alive at Lampedusa, or Ceuta or Arizona
could only hold a lamplight to your heart
You would know the gift of a new day, a drink of water
of refuge from the sun.
May we imagine what we can we give
in our lives mired in property deeds and credit lines
We will never know the force of hunger or the urge to run
or the absolute gold that is every day that awaits you.

Bougainvillea
> *for my brother, Martín*

I.

I cut sprays of bougainvillea
with a steak knife on my lunch break
deep azalea, and flamenco orange.
the vines entangle the iron railing
stretching in garlands that shade
the square of the warehouse porch.

Bougainvillea are free here!
Work has imposed a stoicism
fed by coffee, computer screens
anonymous marketing schmooze
and I hide as music vendor,
publicity coordinator extraordinaire
the import/export foreign port
CD cover queen, e-mail teleport
dream, dream on, move on
pretend no one died,
hold on to your life
where sorrys are swift
people whisper and wonder
why you're back so soon.

On the stairway, around one
sun is high, the best time
for bougainvillea and quiet
so strong, these branches are thick
these thorns amaze me.
I had no idea, all this time
I bought roses.

Bougainvillea who pose and menace,
I am happy now.
as they will stay chaste,
Mini kozo paper lanterns
in fuschia, to wave and hang
over your name.
No one will dare
bend down to kiss your grave.

II.

It is cruel to be buried in a plot
facing the children's section.
The pinwheels and mini balloons
spin and bob the way.
Is this a torment?
Do you see it like I do?

My pain should be less
to see a young couple
at the baby graves
come to see a boy named Elías,
the oval photo reveals his
tender brown face, proud
of Oakland Raiders blacks and greys

Life will trick and cheat you
like a cheap Vegas chapel.
One day you own a Victorian home
You shop for satin nickel fixtures
and custom kitchen tiles
You worry about the trees
who invade your pristine bay view
You have a project to do in the attic
You stockpile sheetrock in the yard
It needed to be hung before it rained.
You should have put it away.

Who would have thought such a hot
October day would be your last?
Orange lavender sunset, so still.
I watched you weld
those ornamental curlicues on
to the iron gates you designed.
That ash red metal could've been a brand
on your muscles: taut canvas
for the gothic heart banner tattoo.
How'd it take them two days
to identify you when your
name was inked on your shoulder?

That's what I remember...
You took off that night.
Everybody told you not to go.

What do you tell a brother
when he drops everything for a woman
he is not supposed to touch?
You drove across the bridge
checked into a freeway-side hotel
and checked out of our lives forever.

The sheetrock crumbles
in February rain.

III.

Bougainvillea are free,
I've run out of money for roses.
Next payday I'll bring tulips
Soon there will be gardenias
from mom's garden,
orchids and hibiscus
I will cut them
and fill the coffee cans.

Bougainvillea are strong
their thorns like nails
to hang themselves on
white villa walls
(like sheetrock new and dry)
like blistering Sevillan patios
and terra cotta planters
of overgrown geraniums
like all the grammas in Mexico had.
Remember our restaurant?
Our big money concept,
our Spanish terrace/bullfight ring?
Live music, family recipes

and top shelf tequila—we'd pack'em in!
With this hope you began to collect
tacky velvet paintings of machos,
mariachis, and sacrificial vixens.
I will inherit them all.

If someone comes to your grave
to press their body close to your name
don't worry these bougainvillea
will ward off feigned praise.
Your visitor will ask
"Who brought these?"
and not know,
not know me, or you
or any of us
well enough to know
who keeps watch to tell
the ill-intentioned, back off
and stay the hell away from my family!

As I drive on Highway 80,
a freeway flash of flames
coursing through my veins
and my limbs feel heat,
I am fast, invisible, and able
to break someone's neck.
I see cars I might follow.
God help me,
I should be at dance class.

I bring bougainvillea
to spend my lunch breaks,
hard commute time,
and some birthday cake with you.
I know it's not really you,
You are rare birds in sunlight
the namesake of my unborn child
the untouched creak on the stairs.

No one will step up to the door
with your weight and rhythm
and fly through the kitchen
for your lunch and an ironed shirt.
I will bring bougainvillea
and nobler flowers when I can,
sorry, but I need to make the rent.

Nature's humor is sick and bent
the same curved talons that
gripped your life, will stubble
the lawn of your grave
and scratch the stone,
and wait and prey
for the insincere...

I'll wait and pray
since I am here.

The Wailing
for the parents who buried their children too soon.

I stood at my brother's burial site and moved
so someone stronger than me
could hold my mother back,
all of her leaning into the lowering
We, the living, there to hold her back

We kept arcing little bits of ourselves
in between the loads of earth
we could not let him go, one more photo, one more rose
a ribbon follows, a child's stuffed tiger, a kerchief,
and hold my mother back

The wailing raged,
more like a freight train,
more like a mother quake, the fault lines of fury collide
a woman who buries a son must feel
those first fetal flutters then full-term feet
to ribs, rewinding ghost baby
threads of milk flow some thirty years later,
counter earth-wise: I fed you to live
You hear all of her
liquefy, unroot
forget the ashes, forget the dust
the universe pulls you inside out
you want to go with your birth blood.

The wailing is all
sound disappears only heaving and heartwork
I see the mothers and fathers in photo stills.
mouths open, a roaring pose
I will not play the clips, I know the sound
a father upright in his bed
4 AM pure rage fills the house
they tagged the son, all hours bereft.

Rage has no words, immeasurable flight
fury moves you, fury follows
the wailing multiplied is this movement now
the will to follow whether son, brother, father

daughter, child, sister, oldest friend
lover you can never become
Keep moving, stay above ground
pace that place and take direction
move the world and let the waves resound

Cara a Cara*

I walked past the pet shop
off Rue St. André des Arts
and turned a corner as if
I knew where to go.
The sidewalk narrowed
now forced off the curb.
I'm shrinking, leaning into the space
between the summer crowds
I caught a hint of you so close
to the eyes of a stranger,
cara a cara, like the fourth *sevillana*
when you hold the pose before spinning
into the end of the dance.

I grazed another man's build,
fixed my gaze on a cyclist's
leg bronzer than my shoulder.
Encircled by glimpses of you
alight with sensation, I believe
in all spliced moments you might be
whole again, to come to me stridently
trying not to laugh, you spot me
before I can see you sayin'
"Where the hell do you
think you're going?"

Like a steel guitar twang
that shot to my stomach
and held me to the fade
I sensed for a demi-second
that you were close.
Elated, so un-earthbound
I was above it all, buoyant
hope is pure light oh, that I would see you here
as a stranger, as a long-ago friend
dizzied in this mazelike city.

I kept that feeling in my pocket
with my blue metro ticket.

I took it to see the masons
build this century's cathedral:
La Sagrada Familia in Barcelona
(that's us, right?)
I could feel you weld there
an ironworker's dream
to pull I-beams for Gaudí
I'm awestruck, yet cursing
the words I won't hear
details only you would know
in new stone of cloistered walls.

You surround me equally in open spaces
so I took that feeling as I ran through
the Causse du Larzac, lunch swinging in a bag,
grasshoppers escape my footfalls.
Heaven is a lemon tart and green, green
apples with all the Roquefort samples
from the villages around St. Afrique
I sat in a valley so flat and quiet
I could only hear a clang of cowbells
and the silence of my own eyelids shut.

Sprinting down a mountain
the feeling overtook me
in a storm that drenched
me three layers through wool socks
boots too heavy to run in,
yet I jet on boulders from the judgement
of thunder slamming down
against each face of the granite mountain.

We are hunted by the boom
dodging rain and lightning, I'm smiling
with alpine rain on my teeth
the wind whips and lashes
it blows tears out my eyes
I will my feet to be native
as chamois hoofing the trail.

If I slip I am gone so instinct leads me
arriving like an arrow
for cover to a grange in Arvieux.

That I might see you
as a stranger in places
we only talked about
while watching races on t.v.
over beers and stale chips,
how this makes me tremble
like our house, when the train,
our little quake, rocked the barstools.

You are with me and alive here
I'm amazed, when I feel you
the first to know the way
you round the corner and have met me
I'm in your arms then you push me
No fear of the fall, you tousle my hair
mid-air, we gasp and taste sky no surprise
we own the same smile and laugh.

Where've you been?

* *Cara a cara: Spanish for "face to face," also a step in a partnered dance from Seville, Spain.*

Playa Cuastecomate
> *for my father, Ramón*

Because there was always your next drink
you did not know my children in your life
They are here to meet you in the waves
here in the blue half-moon cove
where families savor ceviche
cocadas and bocazos de mar
We're here to laugh, roar and run....
You and I laughed rarely
to tear into the waves is joy
I see you in your fishermen's gear,
a travel tube of poles americano style
floral print shirt and huaraches,
you punch your thighs to show me
how strong legs must keep, fuerte así.
I see you, selling baskets of bread as a
a boy, slashing cocos and scamming your next meal
You often told me, don´t turn your back to the sea
and I prayed under my breath, don´t leave us.
I watch my son and daughter now, enter the waves, no fear
me, all edges and wiry fretting,
I wish them some injury, just to know caution
they dive in, venture further into
jeweled surrender that is ancestral
run back to me, touch base at my hip,
my gnarled nerves
keep me from biting the garlic huachinango
from guzzling the icy beer
out of my chair, a rogue wave washes over us,
a rolling wall I am slammed
yet long in my reaching
for air, for image, I scan the surface
spot my boy, where's my girl?
She somersaults out, bobs like a seal
gold flecked face of salt and tears
How far I let them go to know you
in a tender hold of tangled limbs
you were once a child like this
who hungered and huddled
after the tide pulled you in.

Burning Cane

Sweet, acrid burning, I wake from hot sleep,
swing my legs out of a borrowed bed
my feet recoil on the gritty concrete,
toes curled in fear of roaches, chunky as mice
a sunny patio still beckons
through luxury of windows with screens
I sit outside back to the bougainvillead wall,
eyes to the sky then hide from the strangest rain.
Then bow to nature, clasp my ankles,
for the black wispy ashes are floating
like demonic snowflakes, wafting freely
in a see-saw fall at my feet.

A visit in Tuxpan, requires candles at the temple,
glances exchanged with women, huddled at doorsteps
who watch my walk to the cemetery, carnations
and lilies are laid for an abuela I never knew,
she died at thirty-four, kicked by a horse they say
and then her heart exploded
with too much love for a man too far north.

A sign in the plaza alerts volcano activity:
today risk of eruption is low.
Next door the neighbors are chatting,
como amaneció de ceniza,
han de estar quemando caña
so this is cane ash in the tropical plains.
The volcano despite its light plume
like a black-clad mistress of the evening,
spews a thin, deliberate line of smoke.
she is mocking, but will not blow.
The blood of cane is burning here
I'm struck by each lacelike ash, parachute imps
as individual and torrid as a passion intoned.

The day I married in the forest it rained
rain's wet tongue turned to velvet whispers
pink light shown off the cliffs, the ground opalescent
was my jewel, we fled the company of pride.

Friends said "marriage pluvieux, marriage heureux"
but they said nothing about the snow.
The church will fill today in Tuxpan, with mariachis,
compadres, little tokens, lazos and coins.
What do they say of a marriage amid ashes?
Are there benedictions for my sojourn alone?
I catch the ashes in their see-saw fall,
they caress my palm like lucky wishes.
Maybe each one is a desire, a dream in full flight
and expired before I catch it, touch it
before it's gone…who knows what dreams
some women may have, how they die without telling.
Did abuela, too, watch the ashes fall?
Here al pie del volcán, was she patiently waiting
or did she sweep ashes away on the hour,
in front of her clean and godly door?

Everyone asks, "¿Cómo has estado?"
Immediately followed by, "¿Tienes niños?"
According to their sense of nature,
my value as a woman means that
mon petit volcan should've erupted by now.
I should've given birth to a hero, a joy,
preferably a boy to make me proud
who must be paraded around town
and named after the grandfather
who gave the grandmother grief
unspoken tradition calls for boys named Martín.
I think he was a scoundrel.

I will kiss the ashes, face turned skyward
each one a subterranean passion, a secret untold
a testament between worlds and elements
I have touched and spent at least a hundred of these
I want to burn at least a hundred more
let it be soon

In Bermeo at Dusk

Another fishing village
with friends from last weekend,
but Bermeo is in the heart of Euskadi.
It is late March, soft and hazy
from the mist and light rains
over northern Spain this spring,
Country chalets are red monopoly houses
the grasses, a green poker mat over hills.
We buy candy and munchies
from a rinky dink sweet shop.
Pink tubular marshmallows shaped like hams.
They call licorice regaliz
and peanuts are cacahueses.
There is a narrow catwalk bordered by the wall,
the wall barely reaches my waist,
the sea-grey-green it, too, is soft,
but menacing beyond the wall.
Yet the waves leave me unimpressed
 we are too intimate to feign
our surprise and wonder,
each time we meet.

Jorge walks in front of me,
looks over my shoulder
he knows I'm afraid to walk near this wall.
The sea knows I was afraid
to walk along its very shore,
so displaced from my own.
The sea knows how I feared the moon,
how they both witnessed all
and knew my heart, its wanderings
how I cried on the beach in Melaque,
on the pilgrimage we made to Bodega Bay,

the sea knows how afraid
I am to be alone,
yet surrounded by you, always
as I live on this earth.

Old men in boinas
speak gruffly in Euskera,
strange ancient language
of Basque terrorists
and the word *chiquitín*.
Spanish weekenders live in permanence
with something hushed and secret in the air.

I pretend that it's pretty
that I'm glad I came to know it,
but the sea has been in me
since I have loved you
In Bermeo at dusk
it hurts to see it, share secrets,
and walk away.

Ser Madre

Quise ser madre
pero no esperaba noches solitarias
sueño interrumpido por esperar la campanita
de tus llaves en la puerta

Quise ser madre
pero nadie me contó del pánico
al tener una criatura en brazos con fiebre y sarampión
el despertar cada hora para sentir
la leve caída y subida de su pechito
el aliento de su boca, que alivio
cuando le acerco la mano para ver si respira

Quise ser madre
pero no contaba con la fragilidad
de mi cuerpo al darle pecho
y el peso de cargarlo durante el embarazo
y luego fuera de mí, chico muchachón en mi cadera
no sabía como eso iba a aplanar el arco de mis pies
y mandar mis huesos a que se aplastaran
crujientes con dolor en cada paso de mi día

Quise ser madre
pero no me enteré del intercambio:
el tesoro de la mirada confiante de
un niño inocente y la pérdida de tu adoración,
cómo noto tus ojos distraídos
cayendo en otras vistas lejanas.
Mira a esas caritas,
mi propia madre me dice ahora que tengo dos
…ya si eso no te llena el corazón?

Todo el mundo adora a una madre
y su bebé recién nacido
te dicen que es lo mas hermoso de la vida
pero no te cuentan los detalles
los pretextos, los equívocos
que dejan a un niño plantado
en el patio de recreo atascado

en una caja de arena mojada.
Ha llovido y tu no estás pa' recogerlo
por quién sabe qué razón.

Quise ser madre. Soy madre.

To Be a Mother

I wanted to be a mother
but I didn't expect solitary nights
interrupted sleep because I waited for the jingle
of your keys at the door

I wanted to be a mother
but no one told me of the panic
at having a child in arms with fever and rashes
waking at every hour to feel
the light rise and fall of his sweet chest
the breath of his mouth, such a relief
when I near my hand close
to see if he is breathing

I wanted to be a mother
but I didn't count on the fragility
of my body while breastfeeding
nor did I count on the weight of carrying a child
inside me, then outside me, big ol' boy on my hip
I didn't know this would flatten the arches of my feet
that it would command my bones to smash
and crackle with pain in every step of my day

I wanted to be a mother
but I didn't find out about the exchange:
I gained the treasure, innocent child's gaze
and lost your adoration.
How I see your distracted eyes
falling on faraway sights.
Look at these faces,
my own mother tells me now that I have two
…as if that isn't enough to fill your heart?

Everyone adores a mother
and her newborn baby
they tell you it is the most beauty life offers
but they do not tell you about the details
the excuses and the mix-ups
that leave a child stranded

on the playground filthy
in a wet sandbox
It has rained and you are not there to pick him up
for who the hell knows what reason.

I wanted to be a mother. I am a mother.

Just Outside the Gate

You can breathe a cumbia that someone else is bumpin'
It's a summons for your sway, your loose ambling saunter
Qué callejera ésta, mom hisses
cause you're a girl who hangs outside

¿Qué andas haciendo en la calle?
Dejándote mirar
My gaze at strangers when they gaze back
is much too forward
es que también me gusta mirar
…but I'm not just talking bout men,
I love the kids running wild on the sidewalk
in and out each other's houses, improvising
canchas on a not so busy street,
singing to Rihanna on a warehouse pallet,
rigging a swing to a regal tree

I love the viejitos, talking about who
they seen at la pulga, or si
su viejita lo agarró peléndole ojo
a la del security gate en la refinería

I love the 7 year-olds' choreo-magic
meneándose y dando taconazo a la
cumbia tribalera, paletas in hand and
flip-flops not abiding

someone's artful edible salsa
rules the block, I mean roasted soul cleansing
chile guajillo and window sill cilantro
'pa las tostadas comadrita, no seas mala
por qué no invitas….

So much to take in beyond the gate
no me importa que mami me dé una jalada
cuando llegue a casa.
I've seen Yadira, Ixell and Xiomara
these little girls, trading Beanie boos
and homemade bracelets, and their masterpieces

of neon chalk mark the way
to the second grade pachanga
long live the mini callejeras
glad you've learned to play outside

Shine

We say goodbye in the quiet harbor
but it feels more like
Wait, hold me
Which coast will we walk again?

You take my hand and draw
murals inside my palm
Altamira, San Carlos, Lascaux, Lindosa
all the beauty I can feel now

I watch you eat a clementine
you bite it like an apple
I bite a scoop of ice cream this way
because I cannot wait

We are flashes of cinnamon, copper
aurora, burnished Rumorosa, crème brulée
candied ginger, flor de jamaica
colors of cantera stone, boysenberry rose
miel d'acacia, molten gold I am poured of
to hold a jewel of your choice
I will wear you many ways

How to smile at the edge of the world?
Camino sin equilibrio
al compás que solo tú puedes seguir
I put my ear to your chest
as if to a seashell
press my cheek to a cliff
hang on your heartbeat
feel life rush in
the music of so many oceans

Relumbre

Nos despedimos en el puerto tranquilo
aunque se siente más como
espera, abrázame
¿cuándo caminaremos la costa otra vez?

En mi mano dibujas
murales dentro de mi palma
Altamira, San Carlos, Lascaux, Lindosa
Toda la hermosura la siento ahora

Te miro comer una clementina
la muerdes como a una manzana
devoro mi helado así, a mordidas
porque no puedo esperar

Somos relumbre de canela, cobre
aurora, la Rumorosa bruñida y crème brulée
jengibre abrillantado, flor de jamaica,
cantera bajo el río, zarzamora rosa
miel de acacia, oro fluyente
hecha para lucir la joya
de tu gusto, me vestiré de ti

¿Cómo sonreír al borde del mundo?
Camino sin equilibrio
al compás que solo tú puedes seguir
acerco mi oreja a tu pecho
como a un caracol de Tritón
mi mejilla a una barranca
aferrada al latido de tu corazón
siento la vida surgir
la música de tantos mares

January Jicama

I cannot escape your watery crunch
You satiate both thirst and hunger
when slathered with lemon and rock salt,
don't forget the fiery flakes when coupled
with cucumber, an offering straight from
roadside vendors peddling newly
uprooted loot that breaks free from fields.
You are my own water chestnut, finally
a rarity from the earth, you will fly
into markets and magazine pages,
grated and glisten like snowed tinsel, tangy
with blood oranges and spring greens.

With Thanks

Gracias a la vida. These poems have been collected over the past eighteen years. Many of them emerged as I grieved the death of my brother, Martin Del Toro. In 2004, eight years after his death, I was able to publicly read and write about my emotions. As life became more demanding, the immediacy of poetry helped me to cope.

Fuerte agradecimiento to my earliest examples and teachers, Ishmael Reed, Lucha Corpi, Sandra Cisneros and Juan Felipe Herrera. You recognized the poet in me and urged me onward to graduate school and the publishing world. At UC Davis, I was fortunate to study with Sandra McPherson, Pam Houston and the late Marc Blanchard. Thank you for your belief in me.

To my sister scribes and Xingona collective, Suzy Huerta, Aida Salazar, Yaccaira Salvatierra, and Norma Liliana Váldez, you have carried me these past few years and know the depths of the teacher-writer-mamá hustle. Las adoro. Writer and reader friends in the San Francisco Bay Area dazzled me in this journey: James Tracy, Sara Campos, May Castro, Alejandro Murguía, JosiahLuis Alderete, and Joseph Ríos. Gracias for your strong examples: Reyna Grande, Vanessa Hua, Vickie Vértiz, Natalia Treviño, Juan Morales, Estella Gonzalez and Mary Volmer.

Muralistas of the Maestrapeace, Juana Alicia, Miranda Bergman, Edythe Boone, Susan Kelk Cervantes, Meera Desai, Yvonne Littleton and Irene Perez, mil gracias for allowing your art to grace this cover. It can be viewed at www.maestrapeaceartworks.com. Agradecimiento to mentors and inspirations: Norma Elía-Cantu, Helena María Viramontes, Octavio Solis and Luis Alberto Urrea. Thank you to VONA, Bread Loaf, Macondo and Storyknife, my writing families. Gracias to friends and colleagues at Campolindo.

Gracias a mis padres, Ramón y Josefina Del Toro and to my sisters, Mary, Lupe and Marcella.

I thank my brothers, Martin and Raymond for early inspirations. A todos mis parientes en Ciudad Guzmán, Zapotiltic, Tuxpan, Colima, Santa Catarina, Guadalajara y Ciudad de México. Les agradezco tanto a Tía Silvia, Tía Coco, Tía Olivia, Tía Elba y Tía Zenaida.

To my sweet family, Ileana, Lucas and Michel Gasquy, thank you for support and patience. Your coffee, cookies and sustenance help cheer me on. I love you.

Leticia Del Toro is a Chicana poet and fiction writer from Crockett, California. Explorations in Mexico, Spain and France, also inform her work. Leticia's writing has appeared in *Cipactli, Huizache, Zyzzyva, About Place Journal* and more. Her fiction chapbook, *Café Colima*, was published as the 2017 Kore Press Fiction Prize. Additional honors and awards, include a Hedgebrook residency, a Rona Jaffe Award at Bread Loaf and a Storyknife residency. Leticia has also thrived in the writing communities of VONA and Macondo. She holds a B.A. in Spanish Language and Literature from University of California Berkeley and an M.A. in English from the University of California Davis. She has completed a collection of short stories, *Leaving Sugar City*. While writing is her passion, her most creative work is expressed in teaching, motherhood and arts activism.

www.ingramcontent.com/pod-product-compliance
Lightning Source LLC
Chambersburg PA
CBHW022125090426
42743CB00008B/1012